I0821675

CHECKERBOARD BIOGRAPHIES

ALEXANDRIA OCASIO-CORTEZ

RACHAEL L. THOMAS

Checkerboard Library

An Imprint of Abdo Publishing
abdobooks.com

ABDOBOOKS.COM

Published by Abdo Publishing, a division of ABDO, PO Box 398166, Minneapolis, Minnesota 55439.

Printed in the United States of America, North Mankato, Minnesota
052019
092019

Design and Production: Mighty Media, Inc.
Editor: Megan Borgert-Spaniol
Cover Photograph: US House of Representatives/Wikimedia Commons
Interior Photographs: AP Images, pp. 7, 13, 15, 23, 25, 27, 28 (top, bottom right), 29 (top); Shutterstock Images, pp. 5, 9, 11, 17, 19, 21, 28 (bottom left), 29 (bottom left, bottom right)

Library of Congress Control Number: 2019934076

Publisher's Cataloging-in-Publication Data
Names: Thomas, Rachael L., author.
Title: Alexandria Ocasio-Cortez / by Rachael L. Thomas
Description: Minneapolis, Minnesota : Abdo Publishing, 2020 | Series: Checkerboard biographies | Includes online resources and index.
Identifiers: ISBN 9781532119958 (lib. bdg.) | ISBN 9781532174810 (ebook)
Subjects: LCSH: Legislators--United States--Biography--Juvenile literature. | Women legislators--United States--Biography--Juvenile literature. | Democratic Socialists of America--Juvenile literature. | Bronx (New York, N.Y.)--Juvenile literature. | Puerto Ricans--United States--Juvenile literature. | Hispanic American women--Juvenile literature.
Classification: DDC 328.73092 [B]--dc23

CONTENTS

CHAPTER 1

CONGRESSWOMAN OCASIO-CORTEZ

Alexandria Ocasio-Cortez is a political activist from New York City, New York. She is best known for her surprise victory in the 2018 **primary election**. This win led to her election to the US Congress. In 2019, Ocasio-Cortez became the representative of New York's Fourteenth Congressional District.

This district includes the areas of northern Queens and eastern Bronx, where Ocasio-Cortez was born. Ocasio-Cortez was proud to represent her home district. But she was also making history. When she was elected, Ocasio-Cortez was only 29 years old. This made her the youngest woman ever to be elected to US Congress!

Ocasio-Cortez's success surprised politicians. Many hadn't expected her to inspire so much support. Ocasio-Cortez was surprised too. Growing up, she and her family had struggled to make ends meet. Nobody expected a Bronx native with Puerto Rican roots to become congresswoman before her thirtieth birthday!

Ocasio-Cortez is a Democratic Socialist. Democratic Socialists generally believe the government should provide for the basic needs of its citizens.

CHAPTER 2

BETWEEN TWO WORLDS

Alexandria Ocasio-Cortez was born on October 13, 1989, in the Bronx, New York City. Her mother, Blanca, had been born in Puerto Rico. Alexandria's father, Sergio, was of Puerto Rican descent.

Blanca and Sergio moved to New York after getting married in Puerto Rico. In New York, Sergio worked as an **architect**. Blanca worked as a cleaner and secretary.

Much of Alexandria's family had lived in the Bronx for many years. But the Bronx was home to New York's poorest neighborhoods. Sergio and Blanca were concerned about the education available to Alexandria and her younger brother, Gabriel. The couple wanted to send their kids to a school that might provide better opportunities.

Family members helped Sergio and Blanca buy a house in Yorktown Heights. This was a wealthier neighborhood outside New York City. Alexandria moved there when she was around five years old.

Ocasio-Cortez's mother and brother stood by her as she was sworn in as congresswoman.

After moving to Yorktown Heights, Alexandria and her family still visited relatives in the Bronx. Alexandria often observed differences between her new home and the Bronx. She described this experience as "growing up between two worlds." Alexandria soon became aware of how a person's future depends a lot on where she is raised. This awareness would deeply influence her political views later in life.

In Yorktown Heights, Alexandria attended Yorktown High School. She was a driven student who received high grades. Alexandria took a special interest in politics and history. She was known to argue her strongly held political views.

At age 17, Alexandria was accepted to Boston University in Massachusetts. She wanted to study to become a doctor specializing in women's reproductive health. But Alexandria would soon change her course of study. She would also suffer a great loss.

Alexandria's observations of life in the Bronx influenced her future political platform. She would fight for affordable housing and living wages.

CHAPTER 3

SUPPORTING THE FAMILY

In 2008, during the first week of Ocasio-Cortez's second year of college, she received a call from home. Her father was sick with lung **cancer**. He died of the illness that September.

Ocasio-Cortez and her family were deeply shaken by Sergio's death. But the college student channeled her grief into her studies. Despite her personal loss, she excelled at school. She also changed the focus of her studies to economics and international relations.

The Ocasio-Cortez family faced big problems in the years following Sergio's death. Sergio had provided a large part of the family's income. Without him, they were struggling to get by. Additionally, Sergio's death came during an economic **recession** in the US. For several years, it would be much harder to find and maintain jobs.

After graduating from college in 2011, Ocasio-Cortez returned to the Bronx. There, she worked as a waitress and bartender to earn money for her family.

BIO BASICS

NAME: Alexandria Ocasio-Cortez

NICKNAME: AOC

BIRTH: October 13, 1989, New York City, New York

FAMOUS FOR: becoming the youngest woman ever elected to US Congress

ACHIEVEMENTS: winning a **landslide** victory over a well-established candidate in the **Democratic primary election**; winning a congressional election through a **grassroots** campaign led by volunteers

> "The last thing my father had told me in the hospital was 'Make me proud.' I took it very literally."

CHAPTER 4

WORK & POLITICS

For several years after graduating, Ocasio-Cortez concentrated on supporting her family. But she remained interested in politics. Outside of work, Ocasio-Cortez was engaged with US political affairs.

Ocasio-Cortez had gained some experience in politics during her time as a student. In 2008, she had volunteered making phone calls to voters for Senator Barack Obama's presidential campaign. During 2008 and 2009, she had also volunteered for Senator Ted Kennedy, a **progressive Democrat**. Her work as a volunteer involved **immigration** case work and **foreign affairs**.

Ocasio-Cortez loved these experiences. But it was the 2016 general election that drew her into politics for good. That year, Senator Bernie Sanders was running to be the Democratic presidential candidate. Sanders called for a "political revolution" and greater involvement from everyday Americans.

Social movements . . . should be the moral compass of our politics.

In July 2018, Ocasio-Cortez joined Bernie Sanders (*middle*) in supporting Democratic congressional candidate James Thompson (*left*).

Ocasio-Cortez believed in these same values. In 2016, she worked hard to campaign in support of Sanders' nomination.

CHAPTER 5

BRAND NEW CONGRESS

Ocasio-Cortez spent much of 2016 rallying support for Sanders' campaign. In the end, Sanders did not become the **Democratic** candidate. Hillary Clinton was named the presidential nominee in July 2016.

However, the presidency wasn't the only influential position in US politics. There were dozens of other posts across the country that could be filled by **progressive** thinkers. In April 2016, members of Sanders' campaign staff founded an organization called Brand New Congress (BNC). BNC aimed to find and promote people who shared Sanders' progressive views. Then, these individuals could run for Congress in future elections.

In May 2016, BNC founder Saikat Chakrabarti was featured on *The Rachel Maddow Show*. He shared BNC's goal to find new leaders. Soon after, BNC received thousands of applications from interested individuals. One of these applications was from Ocasio-Cortez.

BNC founder Saikat Chakrabarti became Ocasio-Cortez's campaign manager and later her chief of staff.

CHAPTER 6

BNC BOOT CAMP

Ocasio-Cortez didn't think BNC would be interested in her application. In fact, it had not been her idea to apply! Ocasio-Cortez's brother, Gabriel, had sent the application on her behalf. But in December 2016, Ocasio-Cortez heard from BNC organizer Isra Allison.

Allison wanted to know more about Ocasio-Cortez. So, Ocasio-Cortez sent a video of a speech she had given during college. She also discussed her work as a waitress. Ocasio-Cortez explained that working for a small business had helped her learn about labor laws and **immigration**. Allison decided Ocasio-Cortez was a promising applicant.

In the following weeks, BNC invested time and resources into training Ocasio-Cortez. This training included media

THE HOUSE

A congressperson is a member of the US House of Representatives, a chamber of Congress. Each representative serves a specific congressional district for a two-year term. A congressperson's duties include introducing new laws and suggesting amendments to existing laws.

Ocasio-Cortez's BNC training prepared her for the many interviews she would give as congresswoman.

coaching, **debate strategies**, and social media strategies. BNC was preparing Ocasio-Cortez to campaign to represent New York's Fourteenth Congressional District. Ocasio-Cortez had just over one year to persuade New Yorkers that she could be a good congresswoman.

CHAPTER 7

THE FIGHT FOR THE FOURTEENTH

To represent New York's Fourteenth Congressional District, Ocasio-Cortez had to first win the primary election. This election, held on June 26, 2018, would decide the district's **Democratic** candidate. Any new candidates that year would run against the current representative, Democrat Joseph Crowley.

By 2018, Crowley was an experienced and respected politician. Nobody had challenged him in a primary election for 14 years. Many experts thought the district would vote for Crowley.

Crowley also believed he would win. However, Ocasio-Cortez was different from most candidates. She vowed to run a true **grassroots** campaign. A grassroots campaign relies on building enthusiasm among everyday citizens. In contrast, a traditional campaign often relies on money **donations** from **lobbyists** and large corporations.

Ocasio-Cortez's experience as a working-class resident of her district made her relatable to voters.

Crowley accepted almost $3 million in **donations** from **lobbyists** and large corporations. But Ocasio-Cortez refused to do the same. Her campaign was completely volunteer-led. She received about $200,000 in donations, mainly from small contributions.

In the months leading up to the **primary election**, Ocasio-Cortez campaigned hard. In one year, she and her volunteers made 170,000 phone calls to residents of the Fourteenth Congressional District. They also knocked on 120,000 doors and sent out 120,000 text messages.

Several **debates** were organized before the election on June 26. Crowley did not attend the first debate. So, Ocasio-Cortez spoke to an empty chair with Crowley's name on it. Crowley also failed to attend a debate that took place eight days before the election. He sent a representative in his place.

Crowley's absence from two debates made a bad impression on voters.

VIRAL VIDEO

During the primary campaign, Ocasio-Cortez launched a video on YouTube that spread quickly and widely. It showed Ocasio-Cortez interacting with residents of the Bronx and doing everyday activities, such as riding the subway. This established Ocasio-Cortez as a true member of her community.

Ocasio-Cortez's campaign platform addressed issues including climate change, healthcare, and immigration.

Meanwhile, Ocasio-Cortez had earned many supporters. She had reached out to voters old and young. And she had convinced them she was worthy of the district's congressional seat. Ocasio-Cortez won the **primary election** with 58 percent of the vote! It was considered a surprise **landslide** victory.

CHAPTER 8

MIDTERM VICTORY

Winning the primary election made Ocasio-Cortez an overnight sensation. Every major news outlet in the country wanted to speak with the surprise victor. The **midterm election** was quickly approaching. And Ocasio-Cortez had a chance of becoming the youngest woman ever elected to Congress!

The midterm election on November 6, 2018, was another **landslide** victory for Ocasio-Cortez. She received 78 percent of the vote against her competitor, Anthony Pappas. She was sworn in as congresswoman two months later on January 3, 2019.

Some saw Ocasio-Cortez's success as a lucky accident. But others argued that Ocasio-Cortez was exactly the representative her district needed. She had directly experienced the strains suffered by working families in New York. She understood the challenges that residents of her district faced. And she was committed to solving those problems.

After her first month as congresswoman, Ocasio-Cortez returned to the Bronx for a local swearing-in ceremony.

CHAPTER 9

SOCIAL MEDIA MANIA

Since being sworn into Congress, Ocasio-Cortez has continued to attract fans and followers beyond New York. Many of these fans share Ocasio-Cortez's values. These values include **immigration** reform, **green** living, and higher taxation for the wealthy. But Ocasio-Cortez's fans are also drawn to the congresswoman's relatable and youthful energy.

Observers have noticed that young, dynamic politicians such as Ocasio-Cortez are better at relating to young voters. One reason for this is that Ocasio-Cortez grew up using social media. So, she was comfortable sharing her views and lifestyle online.

This openness resulted in the congresswoman enjoying an extraordinary online popularity. On January 16, 2019, she gave her first speech as congresswoman. In just 12 hours, the speech

WORK & PLAY

Ocasio-Cortez often used social media to discuss social issues and economic policy. But she also shared more lighthearted moments, like a video of her dancing outside her office!

Ocasio-Cortez gave her social media followers an inside look at life as a congresswoman.

was viewed more than 1 million times on Twitter. Ocasio-Cortez's own Twitter account had more than 3 million followers soon after!

CHAPTER 10

THE ROAD AHEAD

Ocasio-Cortez has faced criticism and doubt over her vision and goals. Some have described her as unrealistic. Others do not believe her **progressive** approach belongs in the United States.

Political opinions aside, Ocasio-Cortez defied the odds on November 6, 2018. In just two years, she went from waitress to congresswoman. She became one of the most talked-about figures in US politics. And she achieved this by gaining the support of ordinary people.

The 2018 **midterm elections** put more women and people of color into Congress than ever before. Many Americans believed these new leaders represented real change in the US. Ocasio-Cortez is hopeful about future change, saying, "The magic is that it's actually possible."

I really do believe we can live in a healthy, functioning society where people feel comfortable in their ability to go to the doctor, send their kids to college, and save our planet. . . .

In February 2019, Ocasio-Cortez presented the Green New Deal with Senator Ed Markey. This ten-year plan aimed to combat climate change and improve the US economy.

TIMELINE

1989

Alexandria Ocasio-Cortez is born on October 13 in the Bronx, New York City.

2008

Ocasio-Cortez's father dies from lung cancer during her second year at Boston University.

2011

Ocasio-Cortez graduates from Boston University with a degree in economics and international relations.

2008–2009

Ocasio-Cortez volunteers for the campaigns of Senators Ted Kennedy and Barack Obama.

2016

Ocasio-Cortez campaigns in support of Senator Bernie Sanders.

June 2018

New York City's Fourteenth Congressional District votes for Ocasio-Cortez to be its Democratic candidate.

November 2018

New York City's Fourteenth Congressional District votes for Ocasio-Cortez to be its representative in the US Congress.

January 3, 2019

Ocasio-Cortez is sworn in as a US congresswoman.

January 16, 2019

Ocasio-Cortez gives her first speech as congresswoman. In the next 12 hours, her speech is viewed more than 1 million times on Twitter.

GLOSSARY

activist—a person who takes direct action in support of or in opposition to an issue that causes disagreement.

architect—a person who practices architecture, the art of planning and designing buildings.

cancer—any of a group of often deadly diseases marked by harmful changes in the normal growth of cells. Cancer can spread and destroy healthy tissues and organs.

debate—a public discussion about a question or topic.

Democrat—a member of the Democratic political party. Democrats believe in social change and strong government.

donation—something that is given.

foreign affairs—matters relating to international relations and managing the interests of the home country in foreign countries.

grassroots—engaging with or influenced by ordinary people who do not have a lot of money or power.

green—concerned with protecting nature and everything in it, such as the land, sea, and air.

immigration—relating to entry into another country to live.

landslide—an election in which the winner gets a much greater number of votes than the loser.

literal—following the ordinary or usual meaning of the words.

lobbyist—a person who lobbies. Lobbying is trying to influence lawmakers to vote a certain way.

midterm election—an election to select members of public office that takes place at the midpoint of a president's four-year term.

primary election—an election to select candidates who will represent a political party in an upcoming general election.

progressive—believing in liberal social, political, and economic reform.

recession—a period of time when business activity slows.

strategy—a careful plan or method.

ONLINE RESOURCES

To learn more about Alexandria Ocasio-Cortez, please visit **abdobooklinks.com** or scan this QR code. These links are routinely monitored and updated to provide the most current information available.

INDEX